Domestic Abuse:
Our Stories

M . WEBB

PublishAmerica
Baltimore

First printing

ISBN: 1-4137-0720-3
PUBLISHED BY PUBLISHAMERICA, LLLP
www.publishamerica.com
Baltimore

Printed in the United States of America

DEDICATED TO:
MY DAD & MOM, MY BROTHER & SISTER
You've always been my support

AND ESPECIALLY TO:
MY CHILDREN
Your love is my strength

ACKNOWLEDGEMENTS:

First and foremost to Dad and Mom, my brother and sister and my children, I love you all.

To my stepfather, stepmother, sister-in-law, brother-in-law and stepsister; thanks for being part of our family.

To Great-Grammy, Grandpa, Grammy and Great-Aunt Mary, you are not forgotten.

To my good friend Mike M.

To Gail K. for all your help.

To Womens' Shelters everywhere, for helping women and their children to be safe.

To battered women, I hope that you find the strength to leave.

To the women, who didn't make it out, let them not be forgotten.

To PublishAmerica for taking a chance on me.

Domestic Abuse: Our Stories, is a collection of stories based on interviews with women who have been in abusive situations. Fortunately, most of these women are now safe. Although they still live in fear of their husbands or boyfriends (not beating them, but finding them), some of these women found a way out.

If you are in an abusive relationship, you can get out too.

This book cannot tell you *how* some of these women got away, that would only lead their abusers to finding them. Some of the women did not get away from their abusers in time.

But my hope is that this book will encourage women to get away before it's too late.

Doing things legally is always the best way; unfortunately, the legal system doesn't always help, and women are left to use other methods to keep themselves and their children safe.

Keeping women and children safe, should be our biggest concern.

Domestic Abuse: Our Stories

LAUREN

Lauren was a small pretty woman; she taught high school English.

Steve was in one of her classes, he had to repeat 11th grade twice. It's not that he was stupid, he just didn't care. He had a very big crush on Lauren and didn't try to hide it.

Lauren was very careful not to do anything that could be taken the wrong way by Steve. She discouraged all of the advances that he made towards her. She treated him like she treated all of the other kids in her classes.**

One day, Lauren had handed the class back their essays; she was really impressed with Steve's paper. She felt that he had put a lot of thought and research into writing it so she gave him an "A". He was pleased with the grade considering that in all of his other classes he made C's. He felt that maybe she had given him an "A" because she was interested in him.

The next day he asked her about it. She told him that she had no interest in him other than a student-teacher relationship. She explained that he got the "A" because he deserved it, and because he had worked hard on that paper. Steve got upset with her and stormed out of the classroom.**

At around 5:15, Lauren left her classroom and headed for her car in the parking lot. It was winter, so it was fairly dark outside. As Lauren made her way to her car, she jumped back startled when a figure approached her. Then she realized that it was Steve and she relaxed a little.

Lauren asked him what he was doing at the school so late. He forced her to back up against the car. "I thought that you liked me," he said.

"I do like you, Steve, but as a teacher likes her student," Lauren replied. "Nothing more, there can't be anything more."

Steve looked at Lauren for a few minutes then he turned as if he was going to leave. Suddenly he spun around and hit her in the stomach. He picked up a brick block and beat her in the head with it.

Lauren died after the first blow struck her in the head.**

Later that night, the police found Steve sitting next to Lauren's body. Steve has been institutionalized.

ANNIE

My name is Rachel, now. I was once known as Annie; I have three kids. My husband Tom was extremely abusive to me and I left. I ran away, I had no other choice or he would have killed me.

I met my husband when I used to be a cocktail waitress at a bar that he used to go to. At first he was the nicest man, he had a good job, he was funny and sweet. He was also a big tipper!

I was a single mother with two kids. When he met my kids, he was so nice to them. My daughters grew to love him just as I did.

One day he asked me to marry him; he promised that he'd take care of me and my kids. Two weeks later we were married. One month later, I was pregnant. He was so happy. He used to rub my stomach and talk to the baby all the time. He was wonderful to me during my pregnancy.

On the day that our daughter was born, my sister brought my other two kids to see their new sister. My husband grabbed both of my kids by their arms and told them that this baby was number one. My sister and I looked at each other not quite sure that we'd heard him right.

When I got home with the baby it was like a different person lived with us. My older two kids weren't allowed to make any noise, because they would wake up the baby. If the baby did wake up one or both of them would get spanked by him. When I yelled at him, it just made things worse for the kids. He'd get mad at me and hit them harder.

If he came home and the house was a mess, or if the baby was crying, he'd start yelling at me. Soon, he started hitting me. The first time was because he came home and I was still in my robe. He called me a lazy slob and slapped me.

Another time he came home, I was cleaning out a cut that my oldest daughter had gotten from falling off of her bike. He slapped me over and over because the baby was fussing.

It just kept getting worse. If I went out to get the mail, he'd hit me because there were teenage boys next door who would watch me. If the dishes weren't done, if dinner wasn't ready, if the kids had a snack before dinner or if they ate dinner before he got home, I'd get hit. If the baby's diaper was wet, I'd get hit.

He seemed so angry all the time, the only thing that seemed to make him happy was his baby. I threatened to take my kids and leave him, one night after an awful beating. He told me to leave with my kids but that I'd better not take *his* kid.

Things went from bad to worse. One night the kids were all sick and the baby was really fussy. He was mad that the baby wouldn't be quiet so he grabbed her out of my arms. He shook her; he kept shaking her and yelling at her to shut up. This only made her cry louder. I tried to take her back from him but he had a firm grip on her. I pleaded and begged for him to give her back to me.

He got a really strange look on his face, then he threw her onto the couch. She bounced and hit her arm against the wooden arm rest. I picked her up and looked at her arm. It was so red, it had what looked like a welt across it.

I walked up and down the hallway holding her, talking to her and holding ice against her arm. Eventually she fell asleep. I put her into her crib and went to comfort my other two kids who were also crying.

He came in and told them to shut up. They kept crying and cuddling closer to me. He grabbed my oldest by the hair and pulled her up. I kept saying that they were sick and to please stop, but he took off his belt and started hitting her. I tried to stop him but he started hitting me with the belt too. He kept yelling for us to shut up. Finally I guess that he got tired because he stopped swinging his belt.

My oldest daughter lay in a heap on the floor whimpering. I crawled over to her and held her. Something snapped inside me when she asked me why he kept hurting her and why he hated us. I promised her that he would never hurt her or her sisters again, and I meant it. She fell asleep and I carried her into her bed, both girls were sleeping.

I checked on the baby then went into the bedroom to get my nightgown. I thought that he was asleep but I was wrong. He grabbed my arm and twisted it up behind me. Then he put his forearm around my throat.

"I'm leaving you," I whispered.

"Don't ever think that you will leave me. If you try, I will kill you and the girls. You hear me?" he asked menacingly.

Oh, I had heard him alright. He then threw me down onto the bed and roughly pulled at my dress.

"No!" I told him.

"What?" he looked at me surprised.

"I said no!" I sat up on the bed. He pushed me back onto the bed then he punched me in the stomach.

"Don't ever tell me no!" he said.

He put his hands around my throat then he started to choke me. I started to see white spots and heard a pounding in my ears. I pushed at his hands frantically.

"Please," came out as a hoarse whisper.

I thought that I was going to die. I could feel the tears running down my face, my lungs burned. "Please God, don't let me die," I prayed.

Suddenly, he let go of my throat. He pulled at my dress again. He pulled my underwear to the side and tried to have sex. For some reason things weren't working for him. He got off of me, calling me a bitch and punching me in the stomach.

It took me a few minutes to be able to get off of the bed. I grabbed my nightgown and slowly made my way into the living room where I spent the night.

The next day, I woke up before he did. I made myself a cup of coffee and decided that this was it, I was out of here. I couldn't put up with this any longer nor could I put my kids through this. He came into the kitchen.

"You look like hell," he said to me.

I went to the refrigerator.

"I'm not hungry," he said. "I'll pick something up later."

I watched as he walked out the door, then I quickly reached for the phone and called my sister. After hanging up with her, I went to the girls room and woke them up.

We went back into the kitchen and I poured them some cereal. I told them to eat while I went into the other room. I grabbed a few bags and filled them with our clothes. I also grabbed a few of their toys and put the bags by the door.

I got the girls dressed then fed and changed the baby. Just as I was finishing with the kids my sister came into the kitchen.

"Let's go." she said grabbing the bags. I followed her out with my girls.

Twenty minutes later, I was talking to a counselor at the battered women's shelter while my sister watched the kids. The counselor's name was Janie, she looked at all of my bruises and checked my girls too. She also talked to my sister and my girls.

"We have two choices. The first is to go to court and get a restraining order. The second is to go as far away as you can," she said.

"What is a restraining order?" I asked her.

"It is a paper issued by the court, the police get a copy. If he comes within fifty feet of you the police will arrest him."

"Does it work?" my sister asked.

"Unfortunately, not always. Most of the time it doesn't. It's just a piece of paper and the police have to catch him near you. These men get smart and figure out ways around this," she said.

"What would you do?" I asked her.

"I can't make that decision for you. I can only tell you what I have seen. He will probably be allowed visitations with the baby."

"No!" I yelled.

"I know that he's hurt the girls. I believe you, but if he gets a good lawyer you'll have to prove that he hurt the girls and not you." Janie said.

"Of course he did it!" I said. "The girls can tell the court."

"His lawyer will say that you brainwashed them. I've seen this before. Can you afford a lawyer?"

"No."

"We have a lawyer but she has a huge caseload. I don't know how much time she could devote to your case, but she will do her best."

"You don't sound too hopeful," I said sadly.

"I've been here a long time, and I don't want you to think that everything will be easy. It's going to be very hard no matter what choice you make. There is a chance that he won't fight you on anything, but the reality is that he most likely will. You left him, you hurt his pride. Pride is a very big motivator for men!" Janie said, making a few notes in my folder.

"What happens if I leave?" I asked her.

"That won't be easy either. You will have to disappear. He may go to the police and tell them that you kidnapped his baby. You won't be able to contact your family. You, Annie, will disappear. Can you do that?"

"Will I be safe?" I asked. "Will my girls be safe?"

"That depends on how careful that you are. You have to watch what you do. You need to think before you do anything. You can't tell anyone where you are." Janie said.

"Do a lot of women leave?" I asked her.

"Unfortunately, yes."

"Are they safe, do they stay away?"

"I don't know. I don't often hear from them after they have gone,"she said.

"So you don't know how many if any are ever found or worse?"

"No, I'm sorry, I don't. You don't have to decide anything now. You can stay here for up to two months. You are safe here."

"What happens after two months?" I asked.

"During the two months that you are here, we will help you to start the court proceedings. We will help you to get a restraining order. We will go with you to welfare and housing. Beyond that, well it's up to you. We have group counseling sessions, as well as individual sessions. We have workshops on parenting and how to get a job." Janie said standing up.

"I guess for now that here makes the most sense," I said.

"Do you want to be safe? Do you care enough about yourself and your girls to stay away from him?" Janie asked.

"Yes. I won't go back to him, I promised my kids that they'll never get hurt by him again!" I said wiping at a tear.

"Good, you just take a few days. You don't need to go to court yet. Just relax, try to get your head together. Get used to our routine. We'll talk more in a few days. Sound okay?" she asked me.

"Yes," I said also standing up.

"Okay, let me show you were everything is, where you will be sleeping and we'll let you settle in." Janie opened the door. "What does your husband do for work?"

"He owns a home security company," I said.

We walked out into the lounge, we followed Janie from room to room as she pointed out the kitchen, dining room and downstairs bathrooms. They had a big gym and play area for the kids. There was a lounge with lots of couches, offices, a couple of bedrooms and a few unused rooms. There was a room where the housemother slept and a room with two women and a few kids in it.

"This is our day care for our mom's who work," Janie said.

Janie brought us out into the backyard, there were lots of kids' toys there. I noticed that the security system was pretty intense.

"Some security system," I commented.

"We need it. We try to keep our location quiet but because we aren't in a big town, well, people talk," she said.

"Have you had problems?" asked my sister.

"Yes, but the police are very quick to respond, they have to be. We have a lot of women and children here. All of the windows have bars on them and the outside doors are reinforced steel. We have taken everything into consideration." Janie said.

My sister hugged me, "You should be safe here," she said.

"What about you?" Janie asked my sister.

"My husband doesn't put up with much. He and Tom have gotten into it before. I'll be fine," she said.

"Well, let me show you the upstairs," Janie said, climbing the stairs. "We have a chore list. Everyone is assigned a chore for a week. The staff does the grocery shopping although the women make out the menu. We have a room downstairs with clothes and things that have been donated. You can see if anything will fit you and the girls. We have a nurse practitioner that comes in once a week. There are six bedrooms up here, a mini kitchen and two bathrooms.

"How many people are here right now?" I asked.

"Sixteen, plus you four. Twenty today. Although that can change at any time. This is one room." Janie said, opening a door. I looked in and saw six beds, the next room had four beds. Every room had a lot of beds.

"What room do we get?" I asked her.

"We share rooms. I'm putting you in this room with Maggie. She's at work right now, her son is in the daycare downstairs. She goes to class at night so she's not around much. You'll like her, she's very nice."

"I guess that it's okay, but there are only three beds."

"You'll have to double up. They are full sized beds, so two to a bed. It's only for a while. Once a smaller room opens up I can put you in there if you'd like." She said.

She showed me the kitchen and the bathroom. Then Janie and I went upstairs to bring up my bags.

"I'll let you get settled in," she said, as she left. "If you need me, I'll be in my office. Oh yeah, we have bags of diapers and formula in the closet under the stairway. Make yourself at home." Janie left us.

"Well I guess it's not so bad," said my sister.

"No, I guess not. What am I going to do?" I asked her.

"Take a few days to think things over. Don't you even think about going back to him."

"I won't Karen, I promise."

My sister hugged me, "Your going to be okay. You got out of there, that's the most important thing!" she said.

"I know, it's just scary, you know?" I said, lying the baby down on the bed.

"I'll bet. But wasn't it scarier at home?"

I looked down at my other two girls taking their toys out of the bag. "Yes, it was."

"I've got to go. Call me, I love you."

"I love you too, and thanks, sis." I said.

"No matter what you decide, I'll stand by you," she said, as she left.

I watched my sister from my window walk down the sidewalk to her car. She turned, looked up at me and waved. I waved back and watched her drive off.

Janie was right I did like Maggie. She was gone a lot of the time though. I put my kids downstairs in the daycare and went to all the meetings that the shelter had to offer. I even signed up in the gym for a women's self-defense class.

I talked to their attorney too. I had pretty much decided to get a restraining order and file for a divorce. I was determined to fight for my kids.

At the end of the week I called my sister, I needed her to go to my house and get my kids birth certificates and my marriage license. She agreed to go there the next day with her husband. Then she promised me that she'd drop them off.

The next day I told the housemother that my sister was going to be dropping me off some papers. I waited for my sister downstairs and the housemother went to the door when the buzzer rang.

"Hi, Annie. I've got those papers that you wanted." She said coming into the kitchen.

I noticed that she seemed upset. "Are you okay?" I asked her.

"Where are the girls?" Karen asked.

"In the daycare."

"Good, we need to talk." Karen took my arm and we headed for the lounge. After sitting down she said, "Annie, Tom has been calling us and watching our house. I've seen him follow me a few times to the store. He told me that you will come back to him, and next time, you won't leave him. You'll only leave him being carried out. Rick ran him off a few times."

"Did he follow you here?" I asked her.

"No, Rick is outside watching to make sure. Baby, I don't think that he's going to go away," she said.

"What do you think that I should do?"

"I don't know, sweetie. I forgot to tell you that he said that he'll be seeing his daughter soon. He told me that he's gone to court to get custody or visitation," Karen said.

"What?" I stood up. "Custody? He can't do that!" I wiped a tear from my cheek.

"Whatever you do you'd better do it fast. He has a lawyer, Mr. Darnell is his name. He's contacted me trying to find you. He said that he has some papers that he wants to serve you with." Karen told me.

"You didn't tell him where I was did you?" I asked in horror.

"Of course not! I told him that I hadn't heard from you. Oh yeah, your debit card doesn't work. He must have cancelled it. But I have some money that Rick and I came up with for you and the girls." She took an envelope out of her purse and handed it to me.

"He's such a bastard! I'll talk to Janie and the lawyer in the morning." I told her.

"I've got to get going. Call me, okay?" she said hugging me. I walked her to the door and the housemother let her out. "I love you, Annie."

"I love you, too, Karen, and tell Rick thanks. I waved to her as she walked down the sidewalk.

I didn't sleep very good that night, as a matter of fact, no one did. The alarm on the security system kept going off. The housemother called the police and told them to ignore it because it seemed to be shorting out. She also told them that she'd call the alarm company in the morning.

Every time that the alarm went off, it had to manually be reset. I went down into the lounge with a book to read because I couldn't sleep. I told the housemother that I would reset the alarm so that she could stay in bed.

The alarm continued to go off. Each time that it would go off I'd reset it. Around 3 a.m. it went off again. I got up to reset it and thought that I caught a movement out of the corner of my eye. I quickly turned my head, yes, I had seen something. It was a figure, before I could move I heard a familiar voice call to me.

"Annie, you can't hide from me. I'll find you no matter where you go. I'm going to kill you Annie, the first chance that I get. You took away my baby, you bitch!"

I backed up, putting my hand over my mouth. "Leave me alone, please," I said.

"I'm getting custody of my baby, after what you did to her arm! There is a police report filed against you for child abuse. My lawyer was waiting for an address to call the sheriff's department, now we have one. Baby, you screwed with the wrong person!" Tom said savagely.

"You hurt her not me, you won't get custody."

"Can you prove that Annie? I can, the police believe me. The judge believed me too. Just think, by this time tomorrow I'll have my baby and you'll be sitting in jail," Tom laughed.

I heard someone coming down the stairs. I was crying. What could I do? He was right, he'd won.

"Annie?" Maggie called out.

I turned to her then looked outside. Tom was gone. "In here," I said, wiping away my tears.

"What's wrong?" Maggie asked when she saw my tear streaked face.

Maggie led me back to the lounge and I told her what had happened. A few minutes later the alarm went off again. I went to reset it, Maggie followed but waited in the shadows.

"Annie! Annie, why did you leave me?" Tom asked in a muffled voice.

I looked around and saw Maggie leaning forward.

"You are a selfish bitch, a lousy wife and a rotten mother. You really let yourself go, Annie. No man will ever want you. Or are you turning lesbian now, living in a house with a bunch of women?"

Maggie came next to me. "You'd better leave, I'm calling the cops," she said.

"Go ahead, call them. I'm responding to a call that came into my service. A security system problem." He laughed. "How was I supposed to know that my wife was here? What a coincidence."

Maggie and I looked at each other.

"Annie, expect the cops. You did kidnap my child.' Tom turned to go.

I watched him walk away, then I slid down to the floor putting my face in my hands as I cried. Maggie tried to comfort me. How could this have happened? All I did was try to protect my kids and myself. This had all turned around on me! Maggie helped me back upstairs.

At 10:30, I woke up and found a note that Maggie had left for me. She said that she'd fed my kids, brought them down to day care and had let Janie know what had happened last night. I grabbed a cup of coffee and my robe and went down to Janie's office.

"Maggie told me what happened last night, I'm sorry. The sheriff's department dropped off some papers for you this morning. I didn't confirm or deny that you were here. But it seems that you have to appear in court next week to surrender custody of the baby." Janie said.

"So the court believes him?" I asked.

"I called our lawyer and she told me that we don't have any documented abuse, he did. The court has to protect the child. You can try to get the baby put into temporary foster care. But the court has already decided, at least for now, that you can't keep the baby. She will most likely live with him, until he does something stupid."

"But then it could be too late. What if he hurts her again?" I cried.

"I'm afraid for your child, too. But the courts have already decided, for now. You can always go in and tell your side of the story," Janie said.

"If the court is so worried that I would hurt my baby, why have they scheduled something a week away?" I asked.

"He had no address. In a week if you couldn't be served the papers they would have most likely put out a warrant for your arrest."

"What will I do?" I asked.

"You still have two choices. You can go to court and fight it. Or you can leave as soon as possible." Janie said to me.

"He has a lawyer," I said.

"He has a very good lawyer," Janie said.

"I'm leaving, I can't fight him. The court has already decided that I'm guilty. I'm not giving up my daughter. He's crazy!" I said standing up.

"Then you need to leave. Do you have any money?" Janie asked me.

"My husband did something to my debit card, it doesn't work. But my sister gave me $300.00 yesterday."

"Wait here, I'll be right back," Janie said standing up and walking out of the room. I waited with my thoughts. I couldn't understand what was going on. Janie came back into the room and shut the door. "Here's $300.00. That's all that I could get out. I will get some bus tickets for you today. Meanwhile, call your sister, you'll need to say goodbye. Once you leave you can't call or contact anyone from your past. Can you do it?" Janie asked handing me the money.

"I'll have to do it, the stakes are too high not to. I won't lose my kids!"

That day went by, in a blur. I visited with my sister for the last time. Janie gave me some bus tickets and told me where to go.

So, today I am Rachel and I have three girls. It's been six years since I left. Most days I feel safe, some days I relive my life in my mind with Tom. Everyday it gets easier to forget the past.

I still am very careful of what I do or say. I miss my sister very much. I have a job now and am taking a college course. My girls are doing great too. Things look good.

TANYA

My name is Tanya and I have a son. I married my high school crush. From the minute that I saw him, I had such a crush on him. Andy was so cute, he had beautiful blue eyes. He started hanging around a group of guys who drank a lot and were always in trouble. That for some reason made him more appealing to me. I think that it was his bad boy image.

Eventually I'd see him watching me. I would always find a reason to walk by his locker, where the guys hung out between classes. He started to smile at me when I'd walk by or when he saw me in the hallway. My girlfriends and I would laugh when we walked by him and his friends.

I became friends with his younger sister in hopes of being invited over to their house. It worked, I started going over there after school and on weekends. He worked with his father and brothers at their lumber mill. For months we'd flirt back and forth.

One day, he walked by me in school and said that he'd call me later, I was so happy. That night he called at around 8:00, and he told me that he'd pick me up later. I begged and pleaded with my parents to let me go. Finally they agreed, thinking that I was going to visit his brother and girlfriend in town.

Andy drove up in his LTD and I ran out to meet him. We drove down the street and pulled onto a dirt road. He stopped the car and reached over for me. We started kissing, I was so happy to be with Andy, it was like a dream come true! He tried to put his hand inside of my shirt and I told him no.

"Okay," he said, "I'll bring you back home now." If he brought me home now he wasn't going to call me again he told me.

Oh no! I thought, I wanted to be with Andy. I really wanted to be with him. "Alright," I said. He came back over to me again and we kissed. He reached for my shirt, this time I didn't stop him. That night we made love, I was really afraid but he kept telling me that it was okay.

Later when he dropped me off, I asked if he was going to call me the next day. "I don't know," he said, "Maybe." He also told me not to tell anyone about what had happened.

For the next two months he'd call once a week, sometimes twice a week, sometimes every other week. I lived for his phone calls, didn't go anywhere because I didn't want to miss any of his calls. The only problem was that we never went anywhere, only to that dirt road.

At the end of two months, I realized that I hadn't had my period for a while. The next day I told my best friend and we went to the clinic down the road from our school so that I could take a urine test.

The next day, I called the clinic and they said that I was pregnant. Andy called a few days later and after we made love, I told him that I was pregnant.

"I thought that you were on the pill!" he yelled at me.

"Why would I have been on the pill? I was a virgin before I was with you. We didn't do it that often, I didn't think that I'd get pregnant." I yelled back at him.

"Yeah, right," he said putting his head down on the steering wheel.

"You thought that I'd done this before?" I asked.

"Who knows," he said in a muffled voice.

"Andy, I love you," I said.

He put his head up and started the car. "I'll call you sometime," he said.

I started to cry, "What do I do?" I asked him.

"Get rid of it," he said lighting a cigarette.

"Andy! How can you say that? I love you, I want to be with you," I cried, "I thought that you loved me, too."

"How do I know that it's mine?" he asked.

"You're the only one!" I yelled through tears. We drove up into my yard. "Will you call me?"

"Maybe," he said turning away from me. Slowly I got out of the car. He spun the tires as he left like he couldn't get away fast enough.

A few weeks went by and I didn't hear from Andy at all. I decided that it was time to tell my parents. I could have died when I saw the disappointment in my fathers eyes.

My parents went right over to his parents' house. The parents came to the decision that since he was nineteen and I was seventeen that we should get married to give the baby a last name. I was thrilled. I was going to be able to keep my baby and to marry Andy.

My parents arranged for a justice of the peace to marry us, it was a simple thing. No walking down the aisle, no white dress—Cinderella, I wasn't. But at least I got Andy.

Our marriage went from bad to worse fast. Andy didn't want to be married, and he made that clear from day one. He started hitting me and telling me that as soon as I turned eighteen and the baby was born he was divorcing me.

We lived in a dumpy apartment, Andy wasn't home much. He'd come home to sleep and to complain about how fat I was getting then he'd hit me or punch me. He never slept with me either. I tried to be a good wife, I did his laundry, I cooked, I did everything that I thought that a wife was supposed to do.

He just didn't want to be married. I heard that he had a girlfriend but I didn't believe it.

On the night that our son was born, no one knew where Andy was.

When I was ready to leave the hospital, I had to call my parents to come and pick me up. Andy hadn't come to the hospital at all.

"Where's Andy?" my parents asked.

"Oh, he had to work," I said. I was so embarrassed.

When I got home, I settled the baby down and waited for Andy to show up. Finally he came stumbling in at 3a.m. "Do you want to see your son?" I asked.

"No, I don't," he said. I couldn't believe what he was saying. How could he be like that? "The only way to get rid of you is to kill your ass!" he said reaching for his beer. "I'm not getting stuck paying child support for eighteen years!"

I went into the bedroom to be with my baby, not believing the venom that I'd heard in his voice.

The next day after he left for work I called the Women's Abuse Hotline. I made arrangements to go in the following day.

[Unfortunately Andy came home drunk that night and stabbed Tanya numerous times while she was in the shower. She did not survive the attack.

The baby is now living with Tanya's parents. Andy is in prison.

These were Tanya's notes that she had written down in a notebook.]

JESSIE

I'm Jessie, I was married to my husband for ten years. The first nine years were great. We lived in a beautiful house, I had nice clothes, a new car, anything that I wanted he'd give me. But he wasn't home much. I was basically a trophy to him. We went to all of his business functions and I was always the perfect wife.

Then I started hearing talk about his flings, at first I didn't believe it. Why would he cheat on me? We had such a wonderful life.

Time went by and I started noticing little things. He'd tell me that he was working late and if I happened to call the office no one answered. I also started to notice looks from his co-workers. They would look at me sadly then smile when they saw me looking at them.

He couldn't explain his late nights to me. He'd tell me that he was entertaining a client. Where? A restaurant. Restaurants don't stay open until 2 a.m. Oh, we went to a lounge after. I was getting tired of hearing these things.

At one office party I walked into the ladies room and I overheard two women in there talking about my husband.

"I wonder how long he'll keep Rose around," said one.

"Don will trade her in for a new one in a few weeks," said the other one.

"His poor wife, she's such a nice woman."

"Do you think that she knows?"

"How can she not? She's not stupid."

"Thank goodness they don't have any kids."

"Yeah, but Amy swears that she's having his baby!"

"What a mess. Don won't answer any of her calls. She keeps leaving messages!"

"He should have never gotten involved with a eighteen-year-old."

I'd heard enough. I left the ladies room and walked into one of the offices to get my jacket. I headed straight for the door then I had an idea. I went down the hall to my husbands office. I searched through the papers on his desk, I even looked in his trash. I quickly pulled out what I had been looking for. "Don, Amy called again. 555-642-3917. IMPORTANT!"

I put the note into my pocket and left the building. I hailed a cab and went home. I felt tired and physically ill. I got undressed and reached for the phone.

"Hello?" came a sleepy voice.

"Is this Amy?" I asked.

"Who's this?" asked a weary voice.

"This is Don's wife. Are you Amy?" There was silence. "You'd better answer me!" I yelled.

"Yes, this is Amy," she said quietly.

"You've been calling my husband?"

"Yes," she answered.

"Why?" I demanded.

"It's personal," she said.

"Not now! You'd better start explaining things to me real quick." I told her.

Amy started to cry. Between sobs she told me that she had worked at my husbands office. She was a senior in High School and was getting credit through a work study program. She worked there for three months, during that time my husband pursued her relentlessly.

Finally she gave in, then two weeks ago she found out that she was pregnant. She told Don and after that he would never accept any of her calls.

"I'm so sorry. He told me that you guys were having problems and getting a divorce. I would have never done anything if I'd known that you were together," she cried. We made arrangements to meet the next day.

Later, Don came home. "Where did you go?" he asked.

"I felt sick, I had to get out of there." I said not lying.

"You okay now?"

"I think that I'll stay here on that couch for a while. It's easier to get to the bathroom." I said.

"Okay," he kissed me good night. "Can I get you anything?"

"No," I turned over.

The next day, I went to meet Amy. She was so innocent. I wanted to be mad at her but I felt like she'd been taken advantage of. I ended up telling her that if she needed anything to let me know. She told me that she had planned on going to college, I was furious with Don.

That night when Don got home I told him that I knew about Amy. At first he tried to lie about it. Then when he saw that I wasn't falling for it he confessed.

"Maybe this is all for the best. You can't have kids and Amy wants to go to college, let's take her baby," he looked at me innocently.

"What?" I couldn't believe what I was hearing. "Are you missing the whole point?"

"What?"

"You cheated on me!" I yelled at him.

"But I did it for you," he said.

"How could you have cheated for me?" I asked really curious about what his answer would be.

"So we could have a baby."

"No way, Don, you did it for you. You've been cheating on me for how long? How many women have there been? You just got caught this time."I tried to explain.

"But baby, I love you," he said coming over to me.

"Don, I'm filing for a divorce. I'll move out in the morning."

This really upset him. He came real close to me and told me that we wouldn't be getting a divorce. He said that there was no way that I was going to walk out of that door or out of his life! I told him that I wasn't staying and got up.

He pushed me as I walked away from him. I fell against the wall hitting my head pretty hard. He grabbed me by the hair and dragged me into the kitchen.

"You are my wife!" he screamed at me. "You will always be my wife!" He picked up a knife from the counter and held it up to my throat. "If you ever try to leave me I will hunt you down and kill you." The look on his face terrified me.

"Do you hear me?" he yelled.

"I hear you,"I whispered.

"Don't play with me, Jessie! Believe me, I won't hesitate to use this."

I did believe him. I could tell by the look on his face that he was serious.

The next day I moved my things into the guest bedroom. I continued to sleep in there for a few weeks. I guess that he was too preoccupied with Rose' to notice. I made his meals, I cleaned the house, but I tried very hard to stay away from him.

Eventually he'd had enough, one night while I was in bed he came into my room.

"Come to bed," he said.

"I am in bed," I replied.

That made him mad, he jumped onto the bed and straddled me. I could smell the alcohol on his breath.

"Then we'll do it here."

He started to tug at my nightgown. I pushed him and he lost his balance falling onto the floor. I jumped up and ran out of the room. He was right on my heels, he caught up to me and knocked me to the floor. I tried to fight him off but he was too strong.

He pulled at my nightgown, I kicked and scratched at him. He reached for the closest thing that he could find, a metal bat. He started hitting me with it. I rolled onto my stomach and tried to crawl away, then I felt the bat hit my arm and I heard a crunching sound.

I screamed and rolled up into a ball trying to protect myself. That didn't work, his next hit was to my back. Suddenly everything went black.

When I woke up I was in the hospital. The nurses told me that my spine had been crushed by the blow.

Today I am paralyzed and in a wheelchair.

Don is in jail but will be released next year, he had a very good lawyer. I don't know what I'll do when he gets out. I keep getting letters from him saying that he's going to kill me. Amy's been getting letters from him too. As soon as I can get the money together I am moving.

Thank goodness for Amy, she was coming by that night to show him the baby ultrasound pictures. She heard what was going on and called the police.

The police aren't taking any of our letters very seriously. They keep saying not to worry about it, he can't do anything, he's in jail. We know better.

PATTY

My name is Patty, I am a Registered Nurse in the Emergency Room. My husband is the head shift police officer for our local police department.

I met my husband four years ago, he brought a shooting victim into the E.R. We did some harmless flirting at the time. Eventually he got up the courage to ask me out.

Our relationship moved somewhat quickly. We dated for almost a year and then he moved in with me for six months.

We don't have any children, my husband didn't want any. Which is probably a good thing considering how things turned out.

About a year after we were married my husband was promoted to shift leader. He was so happy and I was so proud of him. It meant more responsibility and more pay. It didn't take long for the stress of the job to start to affect him and us. He had a lot of pressure on him, I guess that it was more than he could deal with.

He'd come home and start yelling at me. That started to become an almost daily thing. But I loved my husband and hoped that it was just something that he was going through, I knew that he had a lot of pressure on him.

The first time that he slapped me was because he was upset about work. One of the officers on his shift had gotten reprimanded by the Captain. The officer was caught outside of a woman's apartment near her window. He said that he was urinating.

Anyway, it happened on my husbands shift and he was very upset about it. He came home before I did and was upset that I wasn't there yet. My relief had shown up late, then I had to brief her on what had gone on that day.

So, I finally got home and he yelled at me. He paced back and forth then he slapped me, which surprised the both of us. Immediately, he grabbed me, hugging me and telling me that he was sorry.

For a while nothing happened. Then he started going out for a few drinks with the guys after work. At first things were okay, then he started coming home really drunk. He'd yell at me while following me through the house as I tried to ignore him. If he got mad enough he'd slam me into a wall or push me.

I was getting tired of this and finally stood up to him, telling him that he wasn't being fair to me, or to us. That if the pressure of being a shift leader was too much, go back to being an officer, were you do your shift, then you go home.

This got him very upset. He started hitting me, slapping me, and punching me. When I finally fell to the floor, he left.

Later that night he came home even more drunk.

He came into our room, woke me up and proceeded to beat me and choke me. The whole time yelling at me that I had no faith in him, that I was trying to ruin his career. I guess that he got tired, because just as suddenly as it had started, it stopped. He laid down on his side of the bed and started snoring. I lay in bed awake wondering what was going on with him.

Early the next morning while my husband was still sleeping, I left. I went to the police station to talk to the Captain. I told him what was going on and asked him to talk to Ron. He promised me that he would later that day.

I left to go to work and my day went fine, some of my co-workers asked me if I was okay. I told them that I was.

Ron was home before I was and already on his way to getting very drunk. He was sitting in our living room with his gun in his lap. I leaned down to give him a kiss and he grabbed me by the hair and shoved the gun into my face. He told me that the Captain told him to go home, take a few days off and take care of his problems.

With his right thumb he released the safety on his gun telling me that he sure was going to take care of his problems. I pulled away from him falling back onto the floor. The gun went off missing me.

I stood up and ran from the room. He unsteadily rose from his chair following me from the room. I didn't know where to go! I stood for a second by the hallway trying to decide if I should run to a neighbors house.

Ron came around the corner reaching for me, as he did he lost his balance and fell on the floor, loosing his grip on the gun. I saw the gun fall just as he did, we both tried to get it.

Suddenly he grabbed my foot pulling me. I fell to the ground and he quickly climbed on top of me. He put both of his hands around my throat and started to choke me. I tried to push him off but he was too heavy. Seeing the glazed look in his eyes was so scary. He wanted me dead!

I saw the gun and tried to reach for it, stretching my arm as far as I could. Finally, after what seemed like it took forever I managed to hook my fingers around the barrel of it. I got hold of the gun and meant to just shoot him in the arm so he'd let me go. The gun exploded with such force in my hand, I felt him loosen his grip on my throat, and I dropped the gun.

"You bitch!" he yelled at me. "I'll kill you!"

He grabbed my head and started to pound it onto the floor. The pain was shooting through my body. I could see the blood running down his arm and I could feel it matting in my hair.

He went back to choking me. I felt around for the gun feeling dazed, I found it, picked it up and pulled the trigger. Ron collapsed onto me slowly letting go of my throat. I somehow managed to roll him off of me, and I crawled over to the phone and dialed 911.

I ran my hand through my hair and felt sticky, drying blood. I thought that it was from Ron, later I found out that my head was bleeding.

The police and paramedics came and brought me to the hospital to get stitches in my head. My husband was pronounced DOA. A lot of cops that knew my husband were real upset. I was interviewed by the police and brought to jail.

The next morning the judge let me out on bail saying that I was not a danger to society. This angered a lot of cops because they stick up for and protect their own.

We had a court hearing and with all the evidence from that night, I was released. My husbands death was ruled in self-defense.

As time went by most of the cops let it go. Some of them even apologized to me saying that they should have seen it.

Today, I am still a nurse in the E. R.

41

CARMEN

My name is Donna now, but I was once known as Carmen. I met my husband fifteen years ago. We met through mutual friends, at first I didn't really care for him. He was loud and not very good looking at all. But he kept calling me and showing up at places that I was. Eventually, I got used to him being around.

We started dating and I got pregnant.

One month before my daughter was born, we got married by the Justice of the Peace. I had my daughter and that's when he changed. His family started really bothering me, too.

His two brothers kept having things sent to me, they signed me up for all kinds of mail order things. Then I kept getting all of these bills!

I had some pet rabbits in a cage outside of my house. One day I went to the store, and I came back and they were both dead. Their necks had been broken. I would get phone calls telling me that I was going to die. I once found a dead mouse in my mailbox with a note telling me that I was next. They called the police on me telling them that I locked my baby down in the basement.

My husband started telling me that he was going to get some lye and pour it over me and the baby in the bathtub. That way no bodies would ever be found. I finally got sick of it and threw him out and filed for a divorce.

He started stalking me, if I went to the store I'd see him there. Everywhere I went I saw him. I got a restraining order and found that to be next to useless. The judge told him to stay away from me, he didn't listen at all.

I now think that it was because by marrying him I automatically had an insurance policy taken out on me through his job naming him as beneficiary. There was also a policy taken out on my child after she was born, also through his job.

As soon as he would show up I'd call the cops, then he'd take off. When the cops would finally show up they would tell me that they couldn't do anything unless they caught him there.

I had also gotten restraining orders against his brothers, but they still continued to threaten me. They would call me or leave notes in my mailbox telling me that the Ouija board told them that I was going to die.

I was told numerous times that I was worth more dead than alive. If anything the restraining orders made the family really mad and they did things more frequently. This family was crazy!

The police did catch him and they arrested him about a dozen times. But as soon as he was released he'd do something again or while he was in jail his family would keep calling me saying that my daughter and I were going to die.

The officers were getting tired of coming out and felt that the courts just kept letting him get away with it. Every time that we would go to court the judge would tell him to stay away. But the probate judge told him that he could see my daughter, I didn't let him, I was afraid that he would hurt her or take her.

The whole situation was very frustrating for the police, the court and especially for me.

One day I was on my way to the grocery store and happened to see my ex husbands car. By this time we were divorced, this had been going on for more than a year.

Suddenly the car came up alongside of my car and smashed into me, pushing me off the road and into a ditch. I quickly unbuckled my seat belt and crawled over the seat into the back to check on my daughter in her car seat, I didn't feel any pain at that point.

I noticed movements outside of the car and saw my ex husband walking towards us, I locked all of the doors. He stopped outside of the car and looked inside, raising a gun he pointed it at me. I tried to lean over my daughter to protect her.

I felt a sharp pain in my side, I lay motionless, I think that I passed out. When I woke up, I felt a throbbing pain in my knee and side, it hurt when I took a breath. I looked down and saw that my shirt was soaked with blood. Checking my daughter I was relieved to find her unharmed.

I looked around outside and didn't see any sign of him so I carefully picked up my daughter and somehow managed to half crawl, half walk up the banking to the road. It didn't take long for a car to come. An elderly couple stopped, seeing the shape that I was in the woman took my baby as the man helped me into the backseat.

Feeling safe I again passed out and woke up at the hospital. One of the police officers that had arrested my ex numerous times was there waiting to talk to me. He told me that the bullet had grazed my side and that I was very lucky. I had banged my knee up pretty bad on the dashboard but it should be okay in time. After I told him what had happened he told me that the courts had better listen now. A nurse came in with my baby and the officer left.

When I was released from the hospital a few days later one of the officers picked me up and brought me to my house. He told me that they had towed my car for me and that it was still good to drive.

He also told me that there was a warrant out for my ex but that so far they hadn't been able to find him.

Later that night I kept getting phone calls telling me that next time I wouldn't be so lucky. I called the police and the officer that had been at the hospital came over. He told me that if he were me, because they still hadn't been able to find him, that he'd leave. I thought about that for a few days while the phone threats continued.

I was really scared because they still hadn't found my ex so I decided to pack up and leave. I changed my name and have a beautiful fourteen year old daughter now. I don't know where my ex is but I still keep a watchful eye out. My daughter lives in fear that her father will someday find us. I felt that she needed to know. We are both very careful.

AMANDA

My name is Amanda. I am a police officer and I saw domestic abuse cases almost daily. Not only from on the job, but I, also, had a secret life.

When I would go home my fiancé was very abusive. He worked for the Sheriff's Department at the jail. No one knew that my bruises were from him, they thought that they occurred from the job.

My partner and I transported a man to county jail one afternoon. Tom was working at the jail, and he took the prisoner from us. That was the first time that we met. My partner jokingly told me that there was a man for me, and then he announced that we were going out to Candy's after our shift.

Candy's is a bar that the guys from the police department frequently stop at after a shift. It is a small dingy little bar, but we go there to swap stories and to complain about things. Sometimes a civilian will come in and realize that the place is full of cops and quickly leave.

After our shift Tony, my partner, and I went to Candy's. While we were there, in walked two guys wearing sheriff's uniforms, one was the guy that we'd released the prisoner to earlier that day.

Tony and a few of the guys that we were sitting with started giving me a hard time.

A slow song came on the jukebox, and Tom came over to my table and asked me to dance. After some ribbing from the guys, I accepted. Tom and I walked over to the dance floor, he held me tight and it felt so good, so safe.

A few slow songs later, we were still dancing, Tony came up to me to tell me that he was heading home and that he'd see me the next day.

After a while Tom and I stopped dancing and waked over to a small table. We stayed there talking until Bob, the bartender, came over to us and said that it was closing time. We left and went to an all night diner to continue talking. We were getting along great.

I was surprised to see the sun starting to come up, I hadn't realized that we had been talking for so long. I told Tom that I had to get home and get ready for work. He kissed me goodbye and I drove away.

When I pulled up to my apartment building, I saw Tom in a car behind me. He got out of his car and walked up to me. He told me that he wanted to make sure that I got home okay.

That day at work Tony kept teasing me. He laughed and said that Bob had told him that he had to throw me out so that he could close up and go home.

When I got home from work there were roses sitting outside of my door with a note from Tom.

Later Tom came over and we spent the night together. Our relationship moved very fast, the next thing I knew we were living together, but it felt right.

Tom and I got along great, we understood each others job and seemed to have a lot in common. We always had things to talk about. Soon we were talking marriage, around that time he started yelling at me if he got angry. A few times he had grabbed me by the arm or wrist, I had bruises that I tried to hide from the guys.

Tony and I had been assigned an undercover case in addition to our regular shift. Tom was very upset by this, things started to escalate and he'd get upset more often.

One night at Candy's, Tony saw Tom grab me by the arm and start yelling at me.

A few days later in the patrol car Tony told me that Tom had a reputation at the jail for beating on the inmates, they said that he could get pretty violent. I was too embarrassed to tell him what I was going through at home.

Things kept getting worse at home. Tom was accusing me of cheating on him with Tony. When I told him that there was nothing going on he slapped me and pushed me down onto the floor. We wrestled for a few minutes until I managed to knee him in the groin and get up. He started to come after me and I drew my gun, I told him to get his things and get out. He grabbed his stuff and left, but not before telling me at the door that I was as good as dead. That night I put a chair against the door and slept in the living room.

The next day after work, Tony and I met the guys for drinks at Candy's. I'd told them that Tom moved out but offered them no details as to why he had.

A while later Tom came in and sat at the bar watching us. One of the guys started joking around saying that we'd get back together. I said no way then I went to the ladies room.

When I came out Tom was waiting for me in the hallway. He said that he wanted to get back together, I told him no. He pushed me against the wall and started to choke me.

Tony came around the corner and pulled Tom off of me, a couple of the guys came over, and they led Tom outside. Bob brought me over a cold rag to put against my throat.

Tony came back in, walked over to me and gave me a big hug. He told me not to worry about Tom, he said that they would all watch out for me. The rest of the guys came in and hugged me too, promising me that Tom wouldn't bother me again, the brotherhood of cops.

I've been called out on a lot of Domestic Violence calls but never really saw it from the victims side. I tried to be sympathetic and understanding, now I am. I really feel for these women.

Tom, well, he never comes around me. A few times when he has seen me in a store, he's left.

Tony and I are getting married next month.

JOY

Joy was a 22 year old college student. She met Brian in one of her painting classes. Joy was a quiet, pretty girl. Brian was more outgoing.

They started dating but their relationship wasn't a very smooth one. A few months after they had been dating the Campus Women's Hotline started getting calls from Joy. She asked them questions about her abusive boyfriend. She was told to break it off with him before things went too far.

On Christmas break, Joy was getting ready to go home and Brian was upset with her. He got into her car and told her that he wasn't going to get out. He said that he wanted to be with her for Christmas.

When she wouldn't give in and stay he took a hammer out of his jacket and pulled it back as if he were going to swing it at her face. Then instead he hit her windshield, cracking it.

A terrified Joy yelled at him to get out and started to honk the horn. Brian got out of the car and walked away.

Joy went home for the holidays as she had planned telling her parents that the cracked windshield must have happened at the mall.

When break was over Joy found out that someone had broken into her dorm room. Her things had been moved around but her roommate Tami's things had not been touched. They both suspected Brian but couldn't prove it. Tami begged her to report it, but Joy said that they couldn't prove that it was him and it would just get him madder.

Brian stalked her on campus, begging her to take him back, she always said no, and it embarrassed Brian.

One day while she was waiting for one of the buses with Tami, Brian walked up to her. He asked her to take a walk with him so that they could talk. She told him no, turning away from him, hoping that he would leave.

He pulled out a knife and stabbed her repeatedly while a horrified Tami screamed for help. When Joy's body became still Brian fled. Tami knelt down beside her friend crying.

Brian was later picked up and is now in prison.

Joy was dead at the scene. Tami left school shortly after.

This account was told by Joy's parents, Tami, Brian and Joy's diary entries.

LORI

My name is Lori, I was a waitress at a very popular and busy restaurant. My boyfriend Danny was the bartender. We dated for about seven months and then he moved in with me. We both worked the dinner shift and he often worked until closing.

We got along pretty good for a while until he started coming home at 5 a.m.. Some of the other waitresses told me that Sally, one of the cocktail waitresses, and Danny were spending a lot of time together.

I asked Sally about it, and she confirmed that yes, they were spending a lot of time together. I talked to Danny the next morning and he denied it. So I kind of let things slide for a while.

One weekend, he never showed up at the apartment, so on Sunday morning I drove by Sally's apartment and saw Danny's car.

Monday, I called in sick. That night Danny came home like nothing had happened. I confronted him telling him that I had driven by Sally's and had seen his car.

He started yelling at me, then he picked up my bike. He threw my bike at me, hitting me with it. I yelled at him to leave. He took his things and walked out.

I never went back to the restaurant.

One of the waitresses brought me my last check and told me that Danny had moved in with Sally. She also told me that Sally had a black eye and was crying in the ladies room earlier that week.

MONICA

My name was Monica. I shared an apartment with my best friend Rachel. I was a salesperson in a Real Estate office, and Rachel was a legal secretary.

One Friday night we went out to eat dinner in a restaurant/bar downtown. While we were enjoying our meal, I noticed that a really nice looking guy kept staring at me. He sent over a few drinks then came over to our table and introduced himself as Jim. We all talked for a while, and he asked me to go out the next night. I agreed to meet him at the restaurant.

We had a nice meal but things really weren't clicking for us. He asked me to go out to a movie with him the next night. I said yes, but just as friends. I met him at the theater, he kept trying to put his arm around me, but I felt no chemistry with him at all. He got upset with me, stood up and walked out of the theater. I didn't know what to do, so I stayed and finished watching the movie. When I went out to my car, I didn't notice that I was being followed.

Rachel asked me how my date had gone, I told her what had happened and we both agreed that he was a little off.

Around 3 a.m. there was a loud banging at the door. Rachel and I both went to open it thinking that it was Mrs. Jennings, our elderly neighbor. Rachel unlocked the door and in burst Jim. Rachel and I looked at each other not quite sure what to do.

Jim started yelling about how he had bought drinks, dinner and paid for a movie, he said that I owed him. I tried to explain to him nicely that things just weren't going to work out between us.

He pulled a gun out of his pocket and started shooting calling me a bitch. I watched Rachel fall, then I felt a burning pain in my stomach.

"I hope that you die, you bitch," he said, as he walked out the door.

Mrs. Jennings had called 911, and then she had ran into our apartment. She checked on Rachel, then seeing that there was nothing that she could do for her, she came over to me and held a towel to my stomach.

The rest of the night was a blur, I know that I was rushed to the hospital, then I was rushed in for emergency surgery. They had to remove all of my female organs.

It wasn't until the next day that I found out that Rachel hadn't survived, I felt so guilty.

The police came into my room to talk to me, they told me that they didn't hold out much hope for finding "Jim", if that was even his real name.

Mrs. Jennings also came to visit me. She told me that my purse had been found outside of the building, but that my wallet and keys were missing.

Later that night I received five phone calls, they were from Jim. He told me that I was going to die. He told me that no one rejects him, and that he was going to find me. I called the police and they told me that I would have to wait for him to make a move then they could arrest him.

What? Wait for a crazy man with a gun who'd already killed my friend? No way!

I wasn't going to go back to that apartment, so I did what I had to do, I left.

I am now Stacy. I lost my best friend, I am 22 and will never be able to have kids because of Jim, but I'm safe. At least, I feel safe most of the time.

BONNIE

My name is Bonnie, I have two teenaged sons. Tim is fifteen and Tom is seventeen. I was married for eighteen years, my husband was abusive to me for much of those eighteen years.

I was in and out of shelters with my boys until they wouldn't allow my boys in. They made some of the women feel uncomfortable, my boys were big for their age. I'd go into a shelter, start to pull my life together and then my husband would come around. He'd convince me to try again, saying that eighteen years was a long time to just throw out the window and that my boys needed their dad.

Things would be fine for a while and then something would set him off; he'd start drinking again and then his fists would fly. My boys would try to protect me then they'd get hurt too.

For many years we all suffered the abuse of my husband. He owned a garage in town, he'd have the boys work for him on the weekends and after school. They would change flat tires, and he'd teach them how to work on cars. But he had a very short temper and wasn't a very patient teacher. He'd get upset with the boys and start throwing tools around.

I had no money to leave and no where to go if I did leave him. My husband was very tight with the money, I got just what I needed to run the house, not a penny more.

As time went by the abuse got worse. Our customers got tired of my husbands temper and they would bring their cars to get repaired in the next town. Our garage wasn't doing very well.

My husband got depressed and the violence escalated. He started drinking more and more, we started falling deeper in debt.

One night I mentioned our mounting bills and my husband just lost it. He threw me onto the floor and just started pounding his fists into my head. Tim ran in and tried to pull him off of me. My husband pushed him and Tim lost his balance, slamming into the TV, knocking the VCR to the floor. My son fell to the floor holding his head.

Tom ran into the room after hearing all of the noise. He saw Tim holding his head with blood oozing out from between his fingers. He saw his father sitting on me and hitting me.

He quickly picked up his brothers bat and swung it at his father.

The first blow hit him in the back, the second one hit him across the chest. My husband fell to the floor next to me holding onto his chest.

Tom helped me up and we went over to check on Tim. I grabbed the phone and called for an ambulance. My husband continued to hold his chest making strange noises, but I was more concerned with my son.

When the ambulance came they took both Tim and my husband away to the hospital. Tom and I followed them in our pickup truck.

At the hospital the doctor on duty told us that Tim was going to need some stitches, and that he'd be fine. He said that he'd have to stay the night for observation because he'd hit his head pretty hard.

He also told me that my husband had a massive heart attack and that there was nothing that they could have done for him. He had died shortly after arriving at the hospital.

Bob, the town cop, came over to us. "In my report, he died from a heart attack," he said, putting his arm around Tom.

Tim was released the next day from the hospital.

Today we are running our garage together, I work in the office and do the books and my boys work on the cars. We are very busy now, people are bringing their cars back to us to be worked on. We are finally out of debt.

ANDREA

Andrea worked in a small costume jewelry store in the mall. She also took some classes at the Community College. She was a very pleasant and well liked young woman.

Paula, the jewelry store manager, said that she was always happy and smiling, except when her ex boyfriend would come into the store.She tried to be nice to him, but he would get mad at her and threaten her, all the time. Andrea had become concerned and even asked mall security to walk her out to her car after work.

When the Christmas season came Andrea put in a lot of overtime. Her boyfriends visits became a lot more frequent and a lot more disturbing for Andrea and Paula.

Paula witnessed him push Andrea into a display case, cutting her hand on the edge of it. Andrea told her that he wanted her to come back to him, but that she couldn't deal with his jealousy any longer.

On Christmas Eve, the stores closed early, Andrea said that she would close the store, so that Paula could get home to be with her family.

Mall security had quite a few shoplifters waiting in their office for the police to show up. When Andrea called them to escort her out to her car she was told that it would be about a 45 minute wait. Andrea didn't want to wait that long, she wanted to get home.

A while later one of the employees at J. C. Penny's went out to the parking lot and she remembers hearing a couple arguing there. She didn't pay much attention because she was in a hurry to get out of the cold and to get home.

A few hours later when security made their rounds through the parking lot they didn't hear or see anything unusual. There were a few parked cars there but that was normal, especially in this cold weather.

The mall was closed on Christmas Day.

On the day after Christmas there were many shoppers at the mall to return their unwanted gifts. People were in a hurry to get into the mall and get out of the cold.

Two days later, a woman was standing on the passenger side of her boyfriends car waiting for him to unlock her door. She happened to peek into the car next to them and started screaming.

In the car next to the couple was the body of a woman. Her body was twisted in an unnatural position, you could see that she was dead.

Mall security was called to the scene then they called the police. No one knew why she hadn't been noticed before. Her foot was up over the front seat and her twisted body lay in the back.

Andrea had been stabbed and strangled. Some people think that her boyfriend did it, others think that it was a drifter that killed her.

*This case is still under investigation.

CATHERINE

My name is Catherine, soon I'll be leaving this shelter and my name will be Liz. My boyfriend, Larry, seemed to enjoy hurting me. Punching me and slapping me became an almost daily thing. I still don't know what I did wrong to get him so mad.

At first he told me that I was too pretty and that it would get him mad when guys would look at me. When we would go to the mall he would walk behind me to see how many guys would turn to watch me walk by.

We lived together for a while and then I got pregnant. He started hitting me because I was getting fat.

One day he pushed me down the stairs and I had a miscarriage. Shortly after that I moved out.

He found out where I was staying and started bothering my friends. They got upset because he'd flatten the tires on their cars or smash out their windows. The police weren't much help because we couldn't prove that it was him, and they want to know that they have a case that will stand up in court.

One afternoon when I went outside, he jumped out from behind a car and held a knife to my throat. He told me that he would find me no matter where I went and that I'd better come back to him or he'd kill me because the thought of me with another guy was killing him. I told him that I would go with him but first I had to get my things out of the house. He agreed to let me go and get them once I promised that I would hurry.

Once inside, I locked the doors and called the police. They came and told him to leave the yard because it was private property. He did, he stood across the street. The police said that their hands were tied.

They left and he was really mad, he started calling out to me. Then he started to yell at me that he was going to kill me, that I'd lied to him and was going to be sorry.

I called the Women's Shelter and they told me to come right over. I explained to them that he was waiting outside for me. The woman on the phone told me to sit tight and that she'd send over a police car to come and get me.

A while later, a cop car pulled up into the driveway and I ran out with a few of my bags. I didn't notice Larry following us to the shelter but as soon as the cop left he started banging on the door.

Janice, a worker, called the police. Again they told him to cross the street after the cop left he came back over and started banging on the door again. Janice would call the police but before they would get back there, he had crossed the street and was sitting on a bench.

After a few days of this everyone was getting tired of it. I was afraid to leave the shelter, every time that I looked out the window he was there.

One night Janice came into my room and told me that some of the women were feeling very uncomfortable with Larry standing outside all of the time. He'd even approached some of them and told them to tell me that I couldn't hide forever-that he'd find me wherever I went.

She suggested that I move to a different shelter. I agreed and we made arrangements for one of the women from another shelter to come pick me up.

The next day I had my bags packed and was waiting for a woman named Terry to come and pick me up. Terry was a woman from another shelter. She pulled up into the driveway and came inside. Janice, Terry and I talked about what had been going on with Larry. Janice looked out the window but saw no one.

I followed Terry out to her car, while I was waiting for her to unlock my door I was shoved from behind. It was Larry, he had pushed me then he told me that I was his and that I was never going to get away from me.

Terry came around my side of the car and told him to back away form me as she held out her pepper spray. He backed up and I quickly jumped inside the car, locking the door.

Terry came around to her side, jumped in and we drove off. I heard Larry yelling as we drove away that when he found me he was going to kill me.

When we got to the shelter I settled into my room. Later that night I woke up to the sound of someone yelling outside, I opened the window a little and realized that it was Larry.

The next morning, Terry came into my room and told me that they could help me to get away from Larry. It seemed obvious to her that Larry wasn't going to go away and that the police weren't doing much.

We are going to change my name and Terry said that they will help me to relocate. By this time next week I'll never have to worry about Larry again.

ILENE

My name is Toni, I was once known as Ilene, but that was a while ago. When I was Ilene, I had a horrible marriage. My husband and his family tormented me endlessly. I dated him for seven months, then I married him, his name was Jack. I was two months pregnant at the time. Big mistake!

He used to tell me that I was his, that I was a Philips now. That no matter what, I'd always be a Philips. I really didn't know him very well. You see, I had just gotten out of a six year relationship and I was lonely and unfortunately I jumped right into a relationship with him. Not giving myself any time to grow from the last relationship that I had been in.

My dad told me that I was rushing into things, that I didn't know him. But I didn't listen, now I wish that I had listened to my dad.

Two months after we were married he started hitting me. He would watch porno movies while we were in bed telling me that I was fat or ugly. He'd have these movies on while we had sex.

One night he was pretty stoned and he kept hitting me. I told him that I wanted him to get out of my apartment but he refused. I called the State Police and they told me that if we were married and both of our names were on the lease that they couldn't make him leave. They said that if we were divorced they could have him vacate the apartment.

We were fighting all the time. I was admitted to the hospital because I was having contractions at five months into my pregnancy. The doctors told me that it was most likely due to stress. They said that I needed to get rid of my stress.

I told my husband when I was released that I'd made a mistake and that I wanted a divorce.

"No way!" he told me. "You're a Philips, the baby is a Philips and there is nothing that you can do about it!"

He started to slap me and push me around. I guess that he got tired of it because eventually he stopped. He went to the phone and called his mother. That night his mother and brother, Tom came over.

"You are not leaving this family!" his mother said yelling at me. "You are carrying my first grandchild. You will not get a divorce, you are a Philips for life!" His mother ran that family including both of her married sons lives.

"He hits me, I don't want my baby to have to live this way. I made a mistake, I'm sorry. But I am filing for a divorce." I told her.

She slapped me across the face hard. "You are my son's wife. Frankly I don't care if you are in this family or not. But that baby is ours. When the baby is born, you can get a divorce and leave this family but the baby stays with us. Do you understand?" she yelled at me.

"No, I don't, not at all. You don't own me or my baby. I can leave anytime." I told her.

Her face twisted in rage, she hovered over me. "You will not leave." She slapped me hard. "If you try to leave, you will regret it. Take care of this." She told my husband and Tom. They both came over to me while she watched.

Between the two of them they busted me up pretty bad. Both my eyes were black, my lip was cut, my nose was gushing blood and I had a stabbing pain in my chest when I took a deep breath.

"Don't ever threaten to leave us," his mother told me, pulling me up by my hair. "No one will ever know about this or it's going to be so much worse for you." After saying that she spit in my face. All I could think about was that this family was crazy! Very, very crazy.

Finally his mother and brother left but not before telling me again that I was not to tell anyone what had happened. I laid down on the couch and tried to figure out what I was going to do, I was five months pregnant. My husband went into the bedroom without saying a word to me, he didn't even look at me when he walked by.

I fell asleep, then in the morning my husband went to work without talking to me. I dragged my battered body off of the couch and took a shower. I knew what I had to do.

I called the Women's Shelter and they sent someone to pick me up. Thanks to the shelter by the time that my baby was born I had relocated, had a new identity and was not living in fear any longer.

I guess that Ilene is still married but Toni isn't. I have a six year old daughter now. I don't think that I will ever tell her about the Philips'.

TERESA

My name is Teresa, I was married to my husband for three years, our son was born a year after we were married. During the next two years, he sank into some kind of a dark place. He lost his job and he just couldn't seem to pull himself out of that place that he was in. He became very mean and very violent, He started to hit me quite frequently.

I didn't make much money doing the books for Mr. Sinclair, but it paid the rent and bought the food. We didn't have money for any extras though.

My husband was in need of some professional help, he was becoming more and more depressed. He started yelling at me and our son Todd. If he felt like it he'd hit us. He told me that people were telling him that I was evil. I asked him what people and he told me that the voices were telling him things.

That's when I became very concerned for our safety. One night he told me that the voices told him to kill us all. I finally convinced him not too. I was determined that the next day I was going to find him some help. I checked on my son and my husband and then went to sleep on the couch.

In the morning when I woke up, I was surprised when I didn't hear my son awake and talking to himself. I got up and went over to his bed, he was gone!

I looked through the whole apartment, then I found the note on the refrigerator. He wrote that the voices told him to save Todd and not to worry. I called the police and filed a missing person's report on the both of them.

It's been eight years, my son would have just turned ten. I don't know if he's alive or dead. I wish that I'd gotten my husband help or had left him before this had happened.

JOANIE

Joanie was a beautiful brunette, she worked in the local grocery store. She was a quiet girl, the people that she worked with said that she was a very pleasant person. She didn't date much before she met Adam. She was so excited when he asked her out. They went to a movie and then stopped in for a coffee at Starbuck's.

Joanie had really enjoyed herself. When she went to work the next day she told her co-workers that Adam seemed to enjoy himself also. Later that day flowers were delivered to the grocery store for Joanie. Adam wrote on the note that he wanted to see her again and he included his phone number.

Joanie called him from work but told him that she couldn't see him again until the weekend. He seemed upset but they went ahead and made plans for Saturday night, she also gave him her phone number.

Joanie met him at the restaurant, after eating they decided to go for a walk. Adam asked her if she had cheated on him. Having surprised her she laughed, this really upset him. She changed the subject and they continued to walk. When they got back to the parking lot she told him that she had to go home. He asked her again if she had cheated on him.

"We aren't going out," she replied.

"I'll call you in the morning okay?" he asked her.

Joanie agreed, trying to get into her car so that she could get away from him. He was starting to make her feel uncomfortable.

The next day Joanie's phone rang but she didn't answer it. It just about drove her crazy ringing all day long.

Monday morning she told some of her co-workers about her disturbing weekend. They seemed concerned and told her to stay away from him. When Joanie's shift was over she went out into the parking lot to go home. She noticed Adam leaning against her car.

"You weren't home on Sunday," he said.

"No, I forgot that I had plans," she told him.

"What's his name?" Adam asked.

"It was a woman, Adam. I was with a woman friend. I need to get home." Joanie said trying to get into her car.

Adam grabbed her by the arm. "You cheated on me didn't you?"

"We are not dating, Adam!" Joanie yelled at him, trying to pull her arm away from him.

"You bitch!" he screamed at her. She watched in horror as he pulled a knife out of his pocket and quickly cut her across the neck.

People in the parking lot started screaming. A young man tackled Adam and held him down until the police arrived.

A man and woman went over to Joanie trying to keep her comfortable until the ambulance came.

Joanie couldn't breath, she just kept making noises and clawing at her throat.

She died before the ambulance got there.

MARGARET

I'm Margaret and I was married for under a year. My husband worked in a garage, he was a mechanic. I met him when I was having problems with my car. He seemed real nice at first. We started dating and we had a lot of fun together.

We knew each other for a few years then he asked me to marry him. I agreed and we got married a few months later. Things seemed to go well until I found out that I was pregnant, he was very upset about that. He told me that he wanted me to get an abortion. I told him that there was no way that I could do that. Charlie didn't talk to me for a few days.

He came home from work drunk on a Friday night. "I want you to get rid of it!" he told me.

"No, it's my baby, too, and I want to keep it," I told him.

Suddenly he punched me in the stomach. "Then I'll get rid of it myself," he said, punching me in the stomach, again.

I put my hands over my stomach trying to protect my unborn child. "Please stop!" I pleaded with him.

Finally he did stop. "Will you get rid of it?" he asked me.

"No, Charlie. But I am going to get rid of you!" I stood up and started to head for the door. Charlie came up from behind me and slammed into my back. The weight of him caused me to fall to the ground.

"You won't leave me!" he yelled. He kicked me in the back and stomped on my face.

I guess that's when I passed out, my downstairs neighbor called the police after hearing all of the commotion upstairs.

When I woke up, I was in the hospital and the doctors told me that I had miscarried. From the kicks that I had received to my back, my kidney's were bruised. He had jumped on my arm breaking it in two places. One side of my face was bruised from my forehead to my chin.

The police arrested my husband. In court I was a witness against my husband. He is in prison now for aggravated assault.

KATHI

My name is Kathi, my husbands name is Ronnie, we got married when I was seventeen years old. He was in a band and the guys played in the basement of our house. Sometimes he would go to nightclubs to try to book the band but no one was interested. He would get really frustrated.

The guys would come over on the weekends and they would play for a while then someone would make a beer run, and they would all sit around getting drunk. They'd sit around complaining about how they just couldn't get a break.

One night I told them that if they didn't sit around getting drunk all the time and were serious about making the band work they might get a booking. Ronnie got so mad at me. He stood up, walked over to me and slapped me in front of everyone. I was surprised and embarrassed.

"Don't ever tell me what to do!" he yelled at me.

I ran from the room holding my cheek. Tony followed me out a few minutes later.

"Are you okay?" he asked.

"Yes," I said.

"You are right, we should practice more. No one wants to though, we need to know more than just a few songs, we need to know a few sets." Tony said, putting his arm around me.

"He's so mad all the time." I said.

"He's frustrated, he wants the band to make it. He thought that things were going to take off really fast. There are a lot of good bands out there. We could be a good band if we tried. I've been practicing with some other guys, I may leave these guys." Tony told me.

"I don't blame you at all. I do wish that you guys could make it. You all sound good," I said.

Ronnie called to us from the other room. "What are you two doing?"

"Be right there," Tony called back to him.

We went out into the other room. Ronnie came over to me and gave me a hug. "I'm sorry, babe."

"We really do need to put in more practice time. I like getting drunk as much as the next person, but we've got to get serious!" Tony said to everyone.

They all kept drinking, I got tired of listening to them and went in to bed.

When I woke up Ronnie was standing next to the bed staring at me. "Is everything okay?" I asked him.

"No," he managed to slur.

"What's wrong?" I asked.

"You embarrassed me today," he said to me.

"I didn't mean to embarrass you. I just want you guys to get serious."

"Listen, Kathi, I don't need you to tell me how to run my band."

I sat up in bed. "Ronnie I'm tired of you always drinking and complaining about how you can never make it. You've got to try harder." Ronnie slapped me so hard that I fell back onto the pillows. "That's it! No more," I said, as I got out of bed. When I left the room, I turned and saw Ronnie sit down on the bed. I took a shower, when I was done I went back into the bedroom and saw Ronnie sleeping on the bed.

I packed my things and I left.

CHRISSY

My name was Chrissy. My boyfriend was a violent man, I didn't realize it at first. We dated for quite a while before we moved in together. The whole time that we dated, he was so nice.

I was a bartender and he made deliveries for a beer company, obviously we met at the bar. I moved into his apartment in the Spring. He started out being so charming, then as soon as I moved in he turned into a jealous monster. Every time that I left the apartment, he would accuse me of fooling around on him. Sometimes he would slap me when I denied it.

By the Summer, I was pretty sick of it. So I told him that I was going to move out. He became enraged, he started smashing things in our apartment, and he hit me numerous times.

I ran out into the garage and hopped into my car. I didn't care that I was leaving all of my stuff, I just wanted to get out of there. Just as I started the car, Reg came into the garage. He went over to his workbench and picked something up.

I put the car into reverse, and he came up alongside of me and smashed my window with a wrench. I screamed and pressed down on the accelerator. I threw the car into drive once I got out on the road. He ran behind me yelling that if I left he was going to kill me.

That night, I went to a shelter. The next morning when I called into work, they told me that Reg kept calling for me.

I told the women at the shelter what had happened and they helped me to get away.

Now, I am Anna.

LUCY

My name is Lucy, I met my husband when I was 34 and he was 27 years old. I owned my own house and beauty salon, he was a mechanic. We met on a night that I went out with my girlfriends. He was at the same club with his buddies.

I wasn't dating anyone at the time. I had just broken up with a guy that I had lived with for eight years. I guess that I was feeling lonely, it seemed like all I did was go to work then go home to sleep. I had actually been looking forward to having this night out.

Billy started paying attention to me and I felt flattered. After talking for a while, he asked me if he could have my phone number. I didn't see any harm in it so I gave it to him.

He called me the next day, as a matter of fact, he called me several times that day. We started dating, it was a little hard because we lived forty five minutes away from each other.

Six months later he moved in with me. I wasn't too sure about it, but he kept saying that it was so hard for him to drive that far. We only saw each other on weekends because it was such a long drive.

One month later, I found out that I was pregnant. We quietly married in front of a Justice of the Peace. Things were going pretty well until the in-laws started coming around. The mother was very dominating and forceful, she ran her husband and sons.

Once she found out that I was pregnant, she kept coming around. I liked my space, every week they'd come and invite themselves to stay the weekend.

One Sunday, I told her that sometimes I would like to be able to make plans on my day off. This upset her and she told me that she would decide what we all would do. She said that this was her grandchild and that she was going to be around to watch over things.

We had it out that day, my husband didn't stand up to his mother or back me up at all. I told him that I was going to go away for the few weekend, to avoid them. He didn't want to go because his mother would get mad.

"Fine, stay here. But you really should have backed me up." I told him.

That weekend I went to a motel and caught a movie. On Sunday night, I returned home and they were still there.

"Where have you been?" his mother demanded, slapping my face.

"I had to get away, and I certainly don't have to answer to you! This is my house and I am being driven out of it by you," I told her.

"You are having my grandchild, I have to make sure that everything is okay." she said.

"I know how to take care of myself. I never invited any of you here. I want you to leave and not bother me anymore, you are not welcome here." I told her much to her surprise.

"Billy, you better take care of her. Listen to the way that she is talking to me!" she said.

"Lucy, shut up!" Billy said.

"You've got to be kidding me! You are standing up for your mother! All of you, get out of my house!" I yelled at them.

"You can't throw Billy out, he lives here!" she yelled back at me.

"You listen to me. This is my house and if all of you don't leave now I am going to call the cops," I told them, walking to my phone. I looked at Billy, he stood next to his mother. I dialed 911, a while later the cops showed up and they still hadn't left my house.

The cops told them that if I didn't want them there that they had to leave. At first, he said that he couldn't make my husband leave, but he did strongly suggest it to him.

Finally they left, on their way out the door they told me that this wasn't over. That night they kept calling me.

A few days later they came back and started banging on my door. I called the police and the cops told them to leave. I was told that I could also press trespassing charges against them and get a restraining order.

I went to court the next day and asked for a restraining order. The judge ordered a temporary restraining order, I had to go back in five days to extend it for a year. The head of the probation office told me that the five days was to give the police time to serve them with the papers.

The next day the same cop that had come to my house numerous times showed up at my door. He told me that they had all been served

92

the papers. Then he started asking me a bunch of questions. He asked me if I'd like to go out with him sometime. I wasn't sure how to answer him, I didn't want to get him mad at me so that he wouldn't be there if I needed him, nor did I really want to go out with him. He told me that he'd let me think about it. That night he called me and asked me if I'd decided yet. I put him off by telling him that I just hadn't had the time to think about it yet.

For the next three days he kept calling me and stopping by my house. My in laws kept calling me and so did my husband. I dreaded hearing the phone ring!

Finally, it was time to go back to court. The probation officer, Mr. Harvey, found me in the hallway waiting and offered to let me wait in his office, so that I didn't have to feel uncomfortable out there with them.

I sat down and we started talking, he seemed pretty helpful and sincere. When we went into court, I had to tell the judge what my in laws had put me through, they of course denied it. The judge had a statement from the cop backing up my statement. He agreed to sign the restraining order for one year.

Mr. Harvey brought me out of the court room while my in laws complained to the judge. "The judge is going to sign it as soon as they type it up. It could be a while, if you want, you can go home and one of the officers can drop it off for you later." he told me.

"That would be great," I said.

I left by the side door, Mr. Harvey walked me out to my car. "It's so unfair what they are putting you through," he said. "I wish that I could do something for you."

"You could make them all disappear," I said jokingly as I climbed into my car.

Later that night my husband and in laws showed up at my house. "Get out of here," I told them.

"This piece of paper means nothing," said my mother-in-law. "It can't keep us away."

"I'm going to call the cops," I said.

"You are my wife, if we aren't together you won't be with anyone," my husband said.

"What does that mean?" I asked him.

"You'll see," he said as he turned away from me and walked out.

About an hour later, that same cop that kept asking me out brought me my papers from court. He again asked me out, I tried to nicely tell him that now was not a good time for me to get involved with anyone. I had a lot of things happening right now and hadn't he noticed that I was pregnant?

He said that he was going to keep trying and leaned over and kissed me. I felt very uncomfortable. Thankfully, he left shortly after that, responding to a call.

The next morning Mr. Harvey called me. He told me that he felt very bad for me because of what my in laws were putting me through. Then very quietly he told me that he knew of a guy that could get rid of my husband and in laws.

What? I asked him why he was telling me this, and he told me because he was falling in love with me. He told me that he had already contacted the guy and had a meeting set up.

I couldn't believe this. These were people who were there to serve and to protect. For the next few weeks, I continued to get calls and visits from my husbands and in laws. The police told me that if they weren't hurting me there wasn't a lot that they could do.

When the police did contact them, they were told that they had never called me or even seen me. So it was my word against theirs unless they were caught at my home.

Also, for the next few weeks, I kept getting calls from Mr. Harvey. He would tell me that he had a meeting set up in a motel or that he was going to meet this "hit man" somewhere else. That police officer kept stopping by, too, he'd say that he was concerned and just checking up on me.

I felt really uncomfortable when he would come by, he would always try to kiss me. He was even getting braver, he started backing me up against the wall or a door and touching me. But like he said, who would believe me?

I felt like I should have just shut up and dealt with the in laws every weekend. This was all so overwhelming to me. I kept thinking that if Mr. Harvey was serious and something did happen to my husband or in laws that I would be the most likely suspect.

I did the only thing that I could do. I called the Women's Shelter. I told them everything and they agreed that everything that I said was going to be hard to prove. They knew that these things happened, but it was hard to prove that people with the respect and power that they had would actually abuse it.

Monica, the intake worker, told me that I could try to press charges against them all but I was in for a long legal battle. I talked to her for quite a while. She eventually told me that there was only one way that she knew of to make it all stop. Once the baby came, things were going to get a lot more complicated.

So I listened to Monica and I left. I left everything. I left my house, my car and my salon. I walked away from all of my things. I loaded up two bags and closed out my bank accounts. I lost all of my material things but kept my sanity.

Today, I am someone else. I have a daughter named Cassidy and we are doing great.

AMBER

Amber was a very pretty girl, at 24 she had been living on her own for almost two years. After graduating from the local university, she found a job and got her first apartment. Her mother Janet was so proud of her.

Janet was a single parent and had worked three jobs to put Amber through school. Janet was sure that Amber was going to make something of herself, and not marry a drunk like Janet had.

Amber started working at Telestart, it was a computer company in the area. In the year that she had been there, she had advanced rapidly.

About a month before Amber had died, Janet noticed that her daughter seemed bothered by something. Janet kept asking her if everything were alright.

Finally one night Amber confessed to her mother that she had been dating the boss. She also told her mother that it was a relationship that had to be discreet because he was married.

Amber told her that they had been having some problems recently but that was all that she would say. Janet swore that she saw some faded bruises on her daughter's arms and face.

Over the next few weeks, Amber cancelled all of her lunches with Janet. Janet was very concerned for her daughter; she happened to run into Amber at the grocery store a few days before she had died.

Amber was wearing dark glasses and her silk scarf around her neck. Janet looked at her daughter closely, she asked her to take off the glasses.

What she saw sickened her. Her daughter had a deep cut above her black eye.

"Did your boss do this?" asked Janet.

"It's okay, Mom." Amber said, putting her glasses back on. "Sometimes, I just don't know when to close my mouth."

"Amber, honey, he can't do this to you. Come home with me," I pleaded with her.

"No, we are okay now. I promise. He's coming over tonight for dinner. I think that he's leaving his wife," she said smiling.

Janet tried to convince her daughter to come home for the weekend, but Amber couldn't be swayed.

The next few nights, Janet had a hard time sleeping. She just couldn't seem to shake the feeling that something was wrong.

Not being able to get rid of this feeling of dread, she called Amber's apartment. No one answered all day. That night Janet went to her daughter's apartment, she found that everything seemed to be in order but that her daughter wasn't home. Janet called the police and reported her daughter missing.

The next morning two police officers came to Janet's house. They told her that her daughter's car had been found and Amber had been inside. The cars interior had been set on fire, from what they could tell her daughter had burned to death.

Janet's life fell apart, she found out later that her daughter had been dead before her body had been set on fire. She had died from a head wound, a blow hard enough to crush part of her skull. Then the fire was set to destroy any and all evidence.

Janet knew that her daughter's boss was behind this, but she couldn't prove it. She went to the police with her story of her daughter's relationship with her boss. He of course denied it. He also had an alibi for the time of her murder, he was with his wife.

Amber's murder still remains unsolved.

LISA

My name was Lisa, now I have a new name and a new life. I'd like to know what makes a judge qualified to decide what is in the best interest of a child. The whole time that I was pregnant, I was verbally abused by my husband and his sister. When we split up, they would call me just to harass me.

I had to get a restraining order out against both of them and they continued to threaten me.

When I went before the judge for my divorce, my husband didn't show up. This judge made me wait for almost three hours so that he could call my husband to come.

We didn't own any property or have any kids other than the one that I was due to deliver in three months. When he finally showed up, the judge asked him if he wanted the divorce, he said no. The judge tried to convince me to reconcile. No way, I told him. The next three months the harassment continued.

After my baby was born, we had to go back to court, he was suddenly saying that he wanted visitation rights. During the time that I was pregnant, he had been arrested numerous times for violating the restraining order, by threatening to kill me and my baby.

The judge ordered visitation, I refused. I again reminded the judge that there was a restraining order and that he had violated it numerous times. That judge told me that he was going to allow the visits.

He asked me what kind of father would threaten his own child? Visitation was set for the next weekend. In the meantime, I continued to get threatening phone calls from them. He told me that I was going to lose my baby, that I'd never see her again.

I refused to let him take my daughter, we ended up in court again. I told the judge what had happened again. He said that no one would hurt a baby. He ordered a psychiatric evaluation for both of us and visitation again. That day, I made an appointment for the evaluation.

At my appointment, I talked to the psychiatrist and was evaluated. I picked up a copy of the report a few days later, I also missed the visitation again. My ex husband told me that my baby was going to die. He showed up at my house threatening me again and was arrested.

We went back to court, and I was reprimanded for not allowing the visitation. I told the judge of the threats and the new arrest. I gave the judge my psychiatric evaluation. He asked for my ex husbands and was told that he didn't have it because his insurance wouldn't cover it. Obviously it did, it paid for mine.

My psychiatric evaluation stated that I had some genuine concerns for the safety of my child and myself. It stated that I was an intelligent, thoughtful and caring person. They also suggested that in their opinion visitation should not be allowed because when threats are made against a child, they should be taken seriously.

The judge looked at my evaluation and set it aside. He ordered a lawyer for my baby to supervise in her best interest, and again he ordered visitations. He said that if my husband was saying those things about hurting the baby he was probably just joking. What?

I refused to allow it, and he ordered supervised visitations. My ex husband never showed up for these. What kind of a game was he playing?

We went back into court, between the District and Probate Court; I was exhausted and fed up with the system.

The judge ordered visitations again at a location closer to my ex husband, making it easier for him. That meant that I had to travel for close to an hour to make it easier for my ex because he worked the graveyard shift. My ex didn't show up, again.

I don't know what the problem was but I came up with enough evidence where the judge shouldn't have allowed visitations of any kind. But my ex husbands family had lived in that area for generations, so had the judge's family. Any connection? Why was this judge bending over backwards for him? I couldn't figure it out.

Visitation was set up again. My ex did show up for this one, but sat down looking at magazines and talking to his girlfriend the whole time. As he was leaving, he told me that the first chance that he got, I'd end up buying a baby's casket.

That's it, I'd finally gotten sick of it all. I called the women's shelter. I brought in copies of all of the arrest reports, the complaints, the hearing dates and judgements. I told them my story. They agreed with the psychiatrist, you don't threaten a baby for any reason.

Within a week, they helped me to move.

They obviously saw the urgency in the situation. I do wonder though how that judge would have felt if something had happened. How could he live with himself, and how did he decide what was in my daughter's best interest? The attorney at the women's shelter said, she wondered if the judge realized that he had signed our death certificate.

BRENDA

My name is Brenda, my boyfriend was a hotel manager. I met him at the grocery store in town. He was a really funny guy, I didn't realize that his sense of humor was because of the cocaine that he always used. You would have thought that I would have known that he was on something, after all, I am a pharmacist. I deal with drugs all day long!

I moved in with him shortly after we started dating, his apartment was bigger than mine so it made more sense. Things were going good for a while, at least until the big bosses from the hotel chain started doing an investigation into quality control. They started finding out a lot of things that had been going on. There were rumored cocaine parties held in some of the rooms for the employees, plus the books were always coming up short.

Dylan came home very upset that week. He told me that everyone was trying to get him fired, he started to become very paranoid. He kept saying that some of his employees were making up stories about him.

"Like what kinds of stories?" I asked him.

He told me that they were accusing him of doing drugs and of selling drugs. He said that some of the female employees were lying and saying that he forced them to have sex with him. They were even telling the big bosses that he was tampering with the books and stealing money from the company!

I couldn't believe it. I believed in him, I trusted him.

Mr. Cooper, one of his bosses, called me the next morning. He asked me if I'd come in to talk to him the next day, I said sure, thinking that I could help out Dylan.

That night when Dylan came home, he looked terrible. He said that he was really tired, I guess that the investigation was taking its toll on him. I told him that I was going to talk to Mr. Cooper in the morning. I thought that he would be pleased.

He got so mad at me, he picked up his stereo and threw it at me. Then he turned to me slapping me a few times.

"What are you going to tell them?" he asked.

"I don't know. I was only trying to help!" I said, holding my face.

"Why does he want to talk to you?" he asked.

"I have no idea."

"You better not tell them anything," he said and then he went into the bathroom. I went to listen outside of the bathroom door, that's when I heard sniffing noises. At first, I thought that he was real upset and crying, then I realized that he was in there, snorting cocaine.

That's enough, I thought. I grabbed my purse from the closet and left. I spent the night at my girlfriend's house.

The next day, I did keep my appointment with Mr. Cooper. He asked me if I knew about Dylan's drug use, I admitted that I didn't. He told me that they had a video tape of one of the drug parties that Dylan was involved in. Someone at the party had taped it and then sent it into the Corporate Office.

I'd talked to Mr. Cooper before, he was a very nice man. Both he and his wife had told me before that I reminded them of their daughter. He turned on the TV and VCR, we watched until I couldn't take it any longer and asked him to shut it off.

"You're a nice girl, Brenda, I don't want to see you ruin your life because of him. He isn't worth it, I'm afraid that he'll drag you down, and you've got a lot going for you." Mr. Cooper said, putting his hand on my shoulder.

"I left him last night. I'm not going back," I told him.

"Good. You deserve better. It was actually my wife's idea for me to show you the tape. She asked me to let you see it." he said.

"So, I guess that everything that he said he's being accused of is true." I said.

"I'm afraid so."

Mr. Cooper ended up firing Dylan, and he handed the tape over to the District Attorney's Office. Some of the female employees were pressing charges against Dylan.

I did go back to the apartment and gathered up my things after he went to work.

I still work at the pharmacy, I'm a lot more aware of things now.

DARLENE

My name was Darlene and now my name is Annie. I had to leave my husband before he killed me or my three kids. He kept telling me that he was going to kill us all.

I met my husband when I was 29, and we got married when I turned 30. We had an okay life, nothing exciting but it was alright. I thought that we were doing pretty good, compared to a lot of other people.

By the time that I was 34, I had three kids and no time for anything. At one point, they were all in diapers at the same time. I truly enjoyed my kids, but I guess that I did let myself go.

I stopped wearing makeup, who had time? It was harder for me to lose the weight after my last one. Probably because I had them all so close together, maybe because I was getting older.

I even started to fall behind in the housework. It's really hard to dust, sweep, do the dishes and get the laundry done when there are two toddlers and a baby to care for.

My husband wasn't any help with the kids at all. He refused to change them or feed them. He never even played with them, he just acted like they weren't even there. Although he did complain about how many diapers that I went through. He told me to use two diapers per kid a day. Yeah, that's real realistic!

He would come home from work and complain because sometimes dinner wasn't ready, or the house was a mess. Or his favorite complaint was that I looked awful. I may not have been the best wife, but I was a good mother.

Soon he started calling me a pig, a fat slob, all kinds of things. I started sleeping in with the kids. He didn't even notice for two weeks, that's when he decided that I was good for something.

I tried, I really tried to keep the house clean but as soon as I'd clean up a mess, my two older ones would have two more ready for me to pick up. Or the baby would cry and I'd have to go take care of her.

After the name calling went on for a while, he started to slap me. I wasn't sure what to do then. I guess that I thought that in some way I deserved it. Maybe it happened because I wasn't being a good enough wife.

I started to pick up the house more, I put on makeup again. No matter what I did it just didn't make him happy. He'd still hit me if he got mad.

He kept telling me how it made him sick to have to look at me every day. How I had let myself go and didn't care about how I looked.

His mother also played a very big part in this. She'd come over and just constantly pick and complain about everything. When she wasn't happy, he was even unhappier. When he was unhappy, I was hit.

That woman would come over and point out everything that needed to be done but never once did she offer to give me a hand and neither did he. They would both constantly nag at me. I dreaded it when his mother would come over.

When she would leave, he'd hit me and would tell me how much that I'd embarrassed him. He didn't drink or do any drugs, but he was beginning to turn very violent. I told him that if he'd help me out or not expect so much from me, things might be different.

One Sunday, she came over and I was just so tired of the complaining, so I told her that she was welcomed to help me to pick up. She got really upset with me and we argued. She said that she had raised her three boys and never got any help, that her house and kids were always spotless. My husband stepped in hitting me and telling me to shut up.

"No," I told him. I was sick of them treating me this way.

He grabbed me by the throat and told me that I was more trouble to keep around than I was worth. He also told me that he and his mother had an insurance policy out on me and the kids. We were worth more dead than alive he told me. They both laughed at that.

The next day I went to the Women's Shelter with my kids. They took what I told them seriously enough to get me away from there. Money and greed are big motivators for some people.

My kids and I are safe now.

JANINE

Wanda's daughter Janine met Joe at the grocery store. They started dating and soon Janine found herself to be pregnant. Joe seemed somewhat excited by the news.

Wanda heard rumors that Joe was seeing another girl too, out of concern for her daughter, she told her. Janine confronted Joe and he denied it. This created some friction between Joe and Wanda.

One day when Wanda was driving downtown to a dentist appointment, she saw Joe with a woman. They were standing outside of a restaurant holding hands. Wanda pulled over her car to watch them.

After a few minutes, Joe and the woman walked to a car. She watched as they kissed intimately, then the woman got into her car and drove away. Joe walked back into the restaurant.

Wanda wasn't sure what to do, she knew that she should tell Janine. But her daughter was six months pregnant now and kept having complications. She kept having contractions and was on medication to try to stop them.

Finally Wanda decided that she had to tell Janine. She drove to her daughter's apartment to tell her.

"I thought so," Janine said.

"You knew? How?"asked Wanda.

"We had a fight a few weeks ago because he kept getting phone calls from someone named Anita, she still keeps calling for him. I knew that he was fooling around. He told me that he doesn't want to be tied down with a kid. He told me that he hopes that I have a miscarriage. We had a huge fight and he hit me." Janine started to cry.

"I had no idea. Why don't you just leave him? Come back home. I'll take care of everything." Wanda told her daughter.

"Do you mean it mom?" Janine tried to smile. "I don't want to make things hard for you. I didn't want you to be disappointed in me."

"I want you with me. I want you and the baby safe. You could never disappointment me."

"I'll move back in the morning. I'll tell him tonight. I owe him that much." Janine said.

"Come with me now," pleaded Wanda. "You don't owe him anything."

"I'll be fine, I promise. I'll see you in the morning." Janine said, walking her mother to the door.

That's the last time that Wanda saw Janine alive. The police told Wanda that Janine had overdosed on her medication. Wanda doesn't believe that, when she left her daughter, she had seemed in good spirits. She was happy to be coming home.

Joe was never found guilty.

SARAH

My name is Sarah. My doctors have told me that I'm lucky to be alive. My two children were not so lucky. I don't feel very lucky. I've lost my babies, I would give anything to have them back with me.

Bruce, my husband is in prison now, for two counts of murder and for one count of attempted murder. The police found poison in our milk and some of the other food in our refrigerator.

My husband had taken out an insurance policy on us. He confessed to the police that he had tried to poison us so that he could collect the insurance money.

He never drank milk, so that is how he avoided getting any of the poison. My sons kept getting sicker and sicker. The pediatrician tested them for all kinds of things, but could never pinpoint what was wrong with them.

I had been sick for a few days, vomiting and some pretty bad stomach cramps. One night I heard Kiley making strange noises in his bedroom, so I got out of bed to check on him.

Sammy was moaning in his bed, too; all of a sudden he started to bounce all around on his bed. I found out later that he had been convulsing.

By this time, Kiley had stopped making noises. I thought that he had fallen back to sleep, but I guess that was when he had died. Sammy was really scaring me, I yelled for Bruce. He came into the kids' room, but he was moving real slow and didn't seem too concerned.

I leaned over and vomited, my stomach felt like it was turning inside out. Sammy started to turn blue around his lips.

"Bruce, help him!" I screamed at him.

Bruce slowly lifted Sammy up, he looked at me and carried him into the other room. I got up off the floor and checked on Kiley.

"Oh my god!" I screamed. "Call 911!" I ran into the livingroom and saw Bruce sitting on the couch forcing milk into Sammy's mouth.

"What are you doing?" I screamed.

"He wanted a drink," Bruce said.

He looked unconscious to me. "Are you crazy? What is happening

117

here?" I grabbed the phone and dialed 911.

Finally, the ambulance showed up, they put Kiley and Sammy on stretchers and we left. I rode with my boys, I kept cramping and vomiting so they told me to lie down too.

At the hospital they put me on one of the beds and took a lot of tests. I kept asking how my boys were doing but no one would answer me. They hooked me up to an I.V. and then I fell asleep.

I woke up to find two police officers in my room. One of them saw that I was awake and came over to the side of the bed. He told me that I was safe now, I didn't know what he was talking about. He told me that my husband was in jail and that our milk had tested positive. *What was he talking about?*

The other cop came over and told me that my husband had tried to kill us all with poison. Both of my boys had died but I actually had needed a larger dose for a longer period of time. They had all the evidence that they needed, my husband had confessed and he was going away for a long time.

My boys were dead? I couldn't believe it. How could he kill our beautiful boys? For money?

I have to force myself to get up in the morning. It's been two years since my boys have died and every day I think about them. People tell me that it'll get easier, it hasn't yet. I feel so bad that my boys had to die that way, with so much pain.

> Nearly one-third (31%) of American women report being physically or sexually abused by a husband or boyfriend at some point in their lives according to a 1998 survey.

AFTERWORD

Every eighteen seconds a woman is battered.
The first step in ending the violence is recognition.

Does your partner:
Threaten to hurt you, your children or your family?
Isolate you from friends and family?
Anger easily?
Control finances?
Exhibit extreme jealousy?
Humiliate you?
Destroy personal property?
Hit, punch, slap, kick or bite?

Domestic Violence is a systematic pattern of abusive behavior that may include:
Name calling
Threats and intimidation
Throwing and breaking objects
Isolation and control
Slapping, hitting or punching
Kicking or strangling
Grabbing or pushing
Forced sex
Use of weapons

For more information you can contact: Domestic Violence Hotline

1 - 800 - 799 - SAFE

The author lives in New England with her children.
If you have any questions or comments, you can email this
address and it will be forwarded to the author.
domesticwriter@yahoo.com

Printed in the United States
37841LVS00003B/39

9 781413 707205